THE BLOOM

David Coyle

THE BLOOM

David Coyle

Published by Unsolicited Press
www.unsolicitedpress.com
info@unsolicitedpress.com

Unsolicited Press Books are distributed by Ingram.
Printed in the United States of America.

Developmental Editor: S.R. Stewart
Associate Editor: Chandler S. White
Cover design: Nate Miller

ISBN: 978-1-947021-80-8

THE BLOOM

David Coyle

PART I

The Garden

Unborn, untold, yet-so without youth,
Once formed, unfold, and-so become truth.
Defiant logic, mystique nothing,
Inspired cosmic of unique something.
Time and space unknown then of themselves,
Primal date exploded and compelled.
Ever-unknown to any of eye,
Never had grown many a time.
But came this Universe, fated new,
Its name accrued a verse, dated Bloom.
Beholding countless the precipice,
Unfolding outwards, time's exodus.
Innate conditions of chance and fate,
Dictate provisions in once create.
Relativity reigned ordinance,
Creativity's coordinates.
Incendiary passed physic's laws,
Consequently cast atomics born.
Radiation, gamma x-ray's speed,
Anti-atoms and dark energy.
Intricate sets, probabilities,
Infinite webs, complex destinies.
Parallel timelines and quantum strands,
Unraveled design, forgotten bands.
With-now bound to anew rules enforce,
Went-thou out to due embark its course.
Chaos, it seemed, but still nonetheless,

Came gravity's will to coalesce.
Disruptions from the atoms begun,
They ruptured form in spacetime enough.
Their mass arose dents in the fabric,
Superimposed; sent forth the magic.
Framework laid, first masterpiece came,
Berserk raged, burst from debris to flame.
Clouds of dust, driftings of nebula,
Shrouds of thus gifting spectacular.
Unto darkness, the usual night,
Undo with brightness, refusal light.
So-called were shapes of the soaring arch,
Did fall, this happened; the age of stars.
Sheer nerve of gravity's arrogance,
Veered curves to show off its elegance.
Circles designed pure geometry,
Sacred angles of velocity.
Vast blankets of illuminations,
Lux disbanded in exhalations.
Virgin gorgeousness on virgin felt,
Merging flawlessness, coercion swell.
Starlight shone so white and beautiful,
And inside were atom crucibles.
For stars were the first, but not the last,
Of fires to thirst on death's gleeful path.
Inside they fell, new elements grown,
Collide and swell, these atoms were thrown.
Out into this surging Universe,
Showered through this burgeon interspersed.
Some stars' explosive ends saw evolve,
From supernova events; black holes.
With Universal trend, gravity,

Irreversible bends; galaxies.
With supermassive black hole centres,
Nothing had passage back if entered.
Hundreds of thousands began to twirl,
Upwards of countless of them unfurled.
Their ratios and perfect centres,
Where stars composed of circle vectors.
Grand wheels churned in a slow emergence,
Revealed turns of growing convergence.
Cometh unseen, for none awakened,
If breath had been, it would be taken.
Long slender arms of some eon's length,
With splendour's stars, spun careening went.
Shaped-so with light to be so-admired,
Draped in glowing whiteness spirals.
And in one so-named Via Lacta,
Herein spun so-famed interstellar.
The Sun, or Sol, and its star kingdom,
Begun to mould a planeted system.
Remaining gas and dust gone unused,
To frame en-mass worlds of lasting fuse.
Mercury, Venus, Mars, Jupiter,
Saturn's rings, asteroids, and Neptune.
Of Sol's globes, however, one indeed,
Golden codes endeavoured to succeed.
Earth, the home of, the place of stories,
Worth the throne of, the grace of forming.
A hundred million circles haloed,
This wondrous world in orbit's solo.
Molten lava covered its surface,
But cold eons froze black the furnace.
Earth's radiation sank to black plains,

With amber veins, riverbanks of flame.
But soon dawned time of grand collision,
Loomed and aligned, unplanned, but destined.
Planet incognito hit the Earth,
From it; an obliteration curse.
Shattered back to dust, Earth ripped apart,
But gravity entrusted work of art.
Orbits around the Sun, millions made,
Formed grounded one, satellite of shade.
Ancient companion, mystery alight,
Came in its fashion, gifted in white.
Luna mode, the Moon, the planet's twin,
She slowed the Earth and soothed its wild spin.
The two held in dancing pirouette,
The Moon felled the crescent silhouette.
Earth had tilted in the collision,
Towards seasons instilled, so-given.
The causes here for the falling leaves,
But autumn was still a distant dream.
For the Earth was young and not yet free,
From space's raining comet debris.
But in the falling of these comets,
Came instalments of ice's promise.
Gasses released as the comets came,
And vapours seeped into clouds of rain.
The truest gift was being bestowed,
And through its mist, sleeping ocean sowed.
For millions of years, the waves did crash,
Filling valleys, ravines, each crevasse.
Surface seas were a dead green unclear,
Under iron sky's red atmosphere.
For perfections duty was yet done,

Infectious beauty's cast still come.
Gravity and other rigid creeds,
Harmony's hand in mother's liquid seas.
Sun and Moon soon did their greatest thing,
Ones attuned to boon the native spring.
Rock pools and tides left water to warm,
Uncooled resides witnessed life to form.
Such a thing had never come before,
Once to bring and ever after more.
Enzymes, proteins, mere chemistry,
Fertilised flow and marring entropy.
Singular cells split and multiplied,
Insular gels ripped in germicide.
Bacteria and photo-microbes,
Lacking fear, swept all over the globe.
Organisms of minute affair,
Flourished within time's ruthless snares.
In the chaos for life or death's day,
Championed pharaohs of DNA.
The branches of the great tree of life,
Enchanted each relations divide.
Millions of years, they died and evolved,
Trillions of them retried and dissolved.
Absorb, consume, reproduce, resume,
Adorn tissue to seduce renew.
Swum in the ocean's diversity,
They clung to this potion's nursery.
The atmosphere was yet too hostile,
Life's engineering set too fragile.
Toxic gasses permeated Earth,
Chronic actors to castrate at birth.
The Sun, though kindler, killed indifferent,

No ozone, but some willed persistent.
Draining rock pool tides gave promotions,
Life gained footholds out of the oceans.
Along granite shores, life took to land,
Prolonged invasion, secured withstand.
Clumped together, making living rock,
Slumped and tethered, caked unmoving chalk.
A trillion cells of organic life,
Filling the shores; the stromatolites.
Single cells of unknowing alive,
Shingle films to one growing abide.
Oxygen oozed from stromatolites,
Which resulted in the changing skies.
Stromatolites grew over the world,
Corroded heights, blue skies uncurled.
The seas of green changed in colour too,
Oxygen seeped made them simmer blue.
The Earth was now its distinctive hue,
Its curve endowed with seductive views.
Cracks in the surface, volcanic roar,
Wax lava vented, tectonics sawed.
Magma appeared, cooled, and then hardened,
Lava was smeared, pooled, and made islands.
Continents grew and formed to their shapes,
Oxygen blues, still life cautioned to wait.
Years of orbits faded through timeless,
Menaced hordes of maiden life spineless.
Swam cells, amoebas so-conditioned,
Congealed and endured mass extinctions.
Photosynthesis, consuming light,
Brutal extinctions resumed the fight.
Bacteria's adapted-most grew,

And archaea and eukaryote too.
Volcanic eruptions soon increased,
Caused manic disruptions to the seas.
Carbon dioxide from volcanoes,
Blocked the sunlight and let ice enclose.
Extinction events, came holocausts,
The brinks descended, all near was lost.
Glaciers closed around the equator,
Making frozen life's incubator.
But life survived against hellish odds,
Rightful kinds ascended killing plots.
When the ice retreated to the poles,
Some had survived to defeat the cold.
And-so; life's then powerful moment,
Evolutionary explosion!
Multi-celled organisms evolved,
Bulky shells, gene divisions mould.
Fungi and algae spores reproduced,
Sponges and seaweed, more were induced.
More came; animals, sea worms, and slugs,
With brains, animated squirm begun.
Veteran creatures down in the depths,
Bettering features were inventing sex.
Plant and animals locked in duel,
Stance unfathomable - others fuel.
To claim beyond photosynthesis,
The Cambrian Explosion did this.
Eyes and teeth, instruments for murder,
Size receive meticulous slaughter.
Exoskeletons, the shielding skin,
Endoskeletons, wielded within.
Invertebrates, creatures most common,

And vertebrates, each was unstopping.
Bite and gnash and gouge in poison's game,
Fight and slash about, avoiding pain.
Kill or be killed, hunt or be hunted,
Will for life's skill, stun or be done for.
The Universe was feeling now, this hurt,
It was, now first, reeling its own worth.
Though time was cruel, life didn't give in,
Desired the fuel to motion persist.
Life was rampant in varied domains,
And rife in the planet's ocean waves.
Slim veneer of oxygen prevailed,
Atmosphere, an original veil.
And with this thin band of air to breathe,
Life begun to land sincere from seas.
Creatures soon did swim and crawl the land,
Beaches swooned with fins and claws in sand.
Ignorant, these beasts and plants evolved,
Innocent, tree leaves and roots took hold.
Reptiles, water born and land crawling,
Exiles warred, performed and spawning.
Species rose and their bones rescinded,
Treaties posed between foes unhindered.
Complexity spawned endless vicious,
Aggressively horned menace victims.
Creation was making no illusions,
Nature was as nature is; ruthless.
Eco-systems stampeded valleys,
Epoch rhythms ended families.
Herbivores and terrible beasts roamed,
Dinosaurs, perilous teeth deboned.
For millions of years, these monsters walked,

In brilliant eras, they conquered all.
Insects and plants of enormous size,
Effects of chance and unharnessed time.
Chemistry and gravity's order,
Them unleashed had anarchy lauded.
Hydrogen and helium atoms,
Given time, they let mayhem happen.
This planet, unfurling organic,
Inhabited world of pure magic.
But size wouldn't save the dinosaurs,
They died when it rained a meteor.
The Earth was covered in blackened smoke,
Dinosaurs smothered in rabid choke.
Extinction from comet heaven's fall,
But succinct life dodged this curtain call.
Post-dinosaur and time of monsters,
Host finer crawl, new kinds of conscious.
Pollen flowers seeded hemispheres,
Wanton powers heeded life's big dare.
Birds, mammals inherited the world,
Herds, animals interpret the soil.
Whether not it was bound to happen,
Weather did bring about compassion.
A certain sect of creature so small,
Came intellect bequeathed to them all.
In the land of Africa evolved,
Primate of hand and fires taming bold.
They began to stand on feet upright,
Indeed their flames waned off deepest nights.
Perhaps the earliest to ponder,
At least they were furthest in wonder.
Emergence in the world was unkind,

Superstitious and fearful of mind.
Aware of some inner-God spirit,
They feared the thunder was implicit.
Around them all was this confusion,
Abounded calls, questioned illusion.
Omens bore the curse irrational,
Humans wore the fur of animals.
The need to live forced innovation,
To feed their kin's next generation.
Their bones instinct to outlast the fools,
And with stones and sticks they crafted tools.
They set out on foot across the world,
And decorated with soot cave walls.
Language spoken between these people,
Candid, awoken, seemed less feeble.
Tradition's custom into culture,
Expression's phantom, art, and sculpture.
Their mystic nuance aroused a sting,
Their music announced to them the hint.
Through rhythm and beat they learned to trance,
Groove given to feet, returned the dance.
They knew the truth, though couldn't speak it,
That the Universe flowed between them.
So, from voided void to cusp of love,
The Garden Universe voyaged far.

PART II

The Seed

Come one Mesopotamian night,
A grand feast entertained a tribe.
Camped by a gentle river flowing,
Warm fire against their skins a-glowing.
Smoke billowed up to the stars above,
Folk chatted below, the sounds of love.
Until a storyteller started,
Then fell the curious in silence.
Around the fire, the clan heard the tale,
How for a while, animals were trailed.
The hunters followed footprints and scents,
Finding furs, tree root hints detect.
Tracking some deer to a steep hillside,
Trapping them there, waiting in moonlight.
They slept in a forest overnight,
And kept quiet, awaiting first light.
Then, at dawn's chorus, they left the trees,
Out of the forest's cover of leaves.
With hunger for them to cross their spears,
The hunters' trek near lost the deer.
But at a clearing, the deer were seen,
Drawing nearer, they counted fifteen.
Reliant weapons and men with skill,
With silent gestures, they planned the kill.
With the hunters set in position,
The leader crept without suspicion.
Alas, a fawn and its twitching ear,

Outclassed them all, alerted the deer.
The deer ran fast, the hunters pursued,
Their spears were cast but all were refused.
Only one hunter had held his spear,
Lowly youngster, he was full of fear.
The clan's weakest one, he was its runt,
Chief's youngest son, yearning for the hunt.
Though determined, hunter he was not,
But standing firm, thrower lined his shot.
His spear might've hit, if it had went,
But fear turned fright and his knees so-bent.
A stag with antlers charged right at him,
It ran in anger, fast and thrashing.
Collecting his already thrown spear,
Another hunter aimed at the deer.
Taking down the stag with sharp stone tip,
Making one more stab and fast throat slit.
The hunter successful was named Arn,
The blunderer fearful was named Tar.
Unbelievable but to mother,
Conceived same womb, they were-so brothers.
If brother had not wrestled the wild,
Their father would be bereft a child.
Their father, chief, was known as Baha,
He'd rather weep than sow another.
Telling the story of the slaying,
Arn mocked his younger brother's aiming.
Laughter erupted on the riverbank,
Baha kept silent, for his heart sank.
Tar was silent too, his shame profound,
He kept quiet as Arn portrayed the clown.
"You have no wife to give you offspring,

You have no life within your offering.
Incapable of making pregnant,
Inescapable is your stigma.
Next time, you stay back at camp", Arn said,
"If not, it may be your carcass dead!"
Tar said nothing as the clan chuckled,
His head was low, this king of uncles.
"Enough!" cried Baha, and silence fell,
"There's a place intended for us all."
The clan reasoned chief of the useless,
"He can't even do woman's duties.
The dogs at least guard us while we sleep,
A job we need and thus earn their keep.
No breast nor muscle does he bring us,
Redress sore issue was your promise."
"My son will hold the camp", Baha said,
"While ones, still bold, hunt with me instead."
If not for his father's love and words,
The others' patience would've turned.
Everyone needed to contribute,
Only then could the clan continue.
Tar gave his father a grateful glance,
Both knew this was each their final chance.
For Tar was a burden for the clan,
And time for verdicts were near at hand.
But planned, agreed, they finished eating,
The clan then set in for the evening.
Retreating to shelter in the woods,
Awaiting the felt of nighttime's hood.
Families slept together in warmth,
But loneliness rest for Tar's remorse.
He stayed awake all night with the stars,

In painful heartbreak's delightful scars.
The rushing waters of the rivers,
Crushing torture of his impotence.
Being so worthless was exhausting,
He longed for purpose and belonging.
"When will I find myself?" he wondered,
"When will I be useful to others?"
Listening to the sounds of the world,
Dissonance abound in Tar's disturb.
He found no peace in the swaying trees,
Nor in the leaves in the blowing breeze.
There was no calm in the snoring dogs,
And none had come from the burning logs.
The scent of nighttime's air didn't help,
Descend in the despair of himself.
He thought back to the days of childhood,
Taught the traps and the ways of the woods.
Life had seemed so different back then,
Like a dream of the whispering winds.
He enjoyed hunting with his brother,
They employed cunning with their father.
But one day he was sorely wounded,
And-so; became afraid in movement.
Then came adulthood and its desires,
The sways of womanhood admired.
Alas, he failed to give them children,
Began his days of being haunted.
The trees held less wonder than before,
Valley's coldest afternoons absorbed.
The chirping of the birds felt empty,
A certain horror stirred aplenty.
Sunsets were red but appeared as stone,

Beget to rest dismayed and alone.
Lying solemn on the forest floor,
Crying solace to the horrid more.
He felt his weeping eyes grow tired,
The swell of sleeping sighs acquired.
Sleep would slowly come to him this night,
The wood's lowly hunter did subside.
The breathing of the world so-unveiled,
As leaves falling in the woods inhaled.
In the passage of the wind and time,
In which vanished, dwindled, subsided.
Rock and dirt owing root to the plants,
Of the Earth flowing through time perchance.
Creeks to streams and to rivers in time,
Seeping tree sap to wither the climb.
The beasts beneath the blue skies above,
To each perceive and choose nigh to love.
The birds would fly with feathers on air,
Unlearned defiance measured endeared.
And through the waters swam the creatures,
To ruse, unfaltering the beaches.
And to the wind arose the sunlight,
Renewed begins to follow starlight.
Shadows grew in stones on watersides,
Those in dews and bones brought aside.
In the clouds of nature's circled mists,
Flowers vowed to maker's fertile gifts.
Wood and fire became ashen grey smoke,
Soot and mire, reclaim the ocean's soak.
Hills and grass revealed in open space,
Gills and bark to breathe in token rays.
The energy of the endless flow,

Within its breathing so creatures grow.
In the wild to all learn, reach, evade,
This is how the world turned each new day.
Summer's thirst came in the dusky rain,
Coloured birds with wings to autumn's fade.
The months passed and the hunts did remain,
And-so; Tar kept the clan's children safe.
Clouds and misty droplets of rainfall,
Shrouds of glistening waters downpour.
Time was at once both rapid and slow,
As the undergrowth covered in snow.
The cold of winter's chilling beauty,
Took hold forbidden killing's duty.
In the cold of winter's frozen teeth,
Fell old of clan, to their ends did meet.
Mother of the brothers, Tar and Arn,
Cometh so-hour died in Baha's arms.
Her death hurt only those left living,
Beneath her frozen own forgiving.
Buried not far from the water's edge,
Eternal slumber near riverbed.
The calm rush of the water flowing,
The charmed hush of this daughter's going.
Her favourite fruit was quite ample,
Tar gave her one last one, an apple.
Burying her with the fruit in hand,
Never did he think take root in land...
Rites made sure she made spirits' home,
The site where she was laid marked with stones.
There was little time for any grief,
Fear gave feeble cries and no relief.
For life was death in part and making,

Designed for its depart in shaping.
And life was death like the Sun was Moon,
Evening was become from afternoon.
The clan wandered on, more hunt for food,
Woman and man versus nature's loom.
The skies did pass as the world did turn,
The fight to last continued to burn.
The Tigris River offered them most,
In winter's shivers, transfigured ghosts.
The men went hunting, Tar stayed behind,
Soon boys confronting his lame-confide.
"What is wrong with Tar?" they laughed at him,
"He's not strong enough to hunt with men!"
Tar performed his orders of watchman,
And ignored the taunts of the children.
And in his time guarding those in need,
Began to find curiosity.
In sentry's work, he looked through the trees,
Beyond the bark and to falling seeds.
Leaves of any uncovered displace,
Seeds of varying colour and shape.
"What are these things?" he came to question,
"Their colourings and what intention?
They're everywhere, every plant has them,
They're so widespread, they must do something.
Are they the eyes of the blinded ones,
A way for flowers to see the Sun?
Are they the heart of the bloodless ones,
A way for plants to bleed among us?
Are they the minds of the thoughtless ones,
A way for vines to have consciousness?"
Women picked the seeds to cook and eat,

Along with the leaves and fruits of trees.
But all the while, Tar kept his musing,
Just what they were and of their uses.
The world continued its trance in time,
It twirled in tribute of chance design.
Seasons changed and spring brought some reprieve,
Breathed new babes, in autumn been conceived.
New lives, though they were so very loved,
Applied thorough pressure on the hunt.
More mouths to feed with their women's milk,
Obliged new need to ascertain kills.
And though no children had come from him,
Tar loved each and every one of them.
With none of his own making to care,
Begun something of thinking compare.
"So small, with helpless cries of impulse,
Like all the selfish sighs of adults.
Their little hands and their little feet,
Like brittle bands of air which to breathe.
They need us more than anything else,
Because they cannot fend for themselves.
But who needs the other more?" Tar questioned,
"Unto deeds of ours their direction.
Without them, we have no such purpose,
Undoubtedly, make us so-worthless.
And this is why I have no meaning,
Forgiveness is my only seeking."
One of these gorgeous new born babies,
Was Tar's niece, born in the Euphrates.
Her eyes were blue as the sky above,
Her mother, Alu, did-so cry with love.
In the basic words of their language,

Bestowed a name that meant 'courageous'.
His brother, Arn, and Alu did weep,
They loved Saha more than days to keep.
And when first Tar held her in his arms,
She mended his heart and gave him calm.
Arn then asked Tar to defend his girl,
"Your new task, brother, protect her world."
And to this end, Tar made promise-pledge,
"I'll so-defend her grace to my death."
The days of spring passed by into nights,
Rephrased a bringing of warmer lights.
The days grew longer and slowed in ease,
Arranged the summer lands growing green.
More animals came back to the land,
So easier to track for the clan.
Every day, the hunter's made a kill,
In this way, the clan had of their fill.
They were respectful of the wild beasts,
Each herd attentive to their child feasts.
But evil comes not from animals,
Its shape human; them so natural.
For came an evening of warm summer,
And Tar fell sleeping on heat's number.
His only job had been forgotten,
This timely loss - unseen some robbers.
A raiding party crept up slow,
The canine out hunting would've known.
But alas, without them, no alarm,
Nor Tar's witness welcomed coming harm.
Men of hunger and winter's victim,
Ten in number, no kids or women.
The fate of the world was cruel to them,

It made them cold and brutal within.
Their terror was swift and forsaken,
Children were killed and women taken.
Did take the shrieking and children's screams,
To shake the creaking of Tar's dull dreams.
By the time he realised what had past,
Only five terrorised kids were last.
Two women remained, they were dismayed,
The children were maimed, their tender babes.
The raiders spared only those unseen,
They'd slain the rest with their clubs obscene.
Survivors cried in distraught silence,
While others died from this brought violence.
Had Tar been there, he'd have surely died,
But with warning, more might've survived.
Wails filled the clan's broken disbelief,
Failed was man's coping for such grief.
Then fell ruin upon this brittle world,
Tar saw strewn his brother's little girl.
With finely bloodied gashes of red,
Her tiny body was smashed to death.
Her blue eyes now like the daytime moon,
A demise of life that came too soon.
Her disembodied, mangled, lifeless harmed,
Her limp body dangled in his arms.
Lying nearby was her dead mother,
Who died defending her child's honour.
Numbness overcame Tar, some horror felt,
Thunder couldn't sway him from his guilt.
Blood-red stained the ground and fire pit,
Clubbed dead and pained around did dire sit.
The women cuddled the dead and wailed,

The children huddled in fear exhaled.
Tar sat motionless in dazed despair,
And at hopelessness, enslaved, ensnared.
The grief made his bones feel warm and numb,
He heaved in his own reeling become.
Time seemed to freeze in a static pain,
The leaves to breeze in wind's panicked frame.
Cold water drowned him in affliction,
Arn's daughter crowned in death's conviction.
Tar's muscles tightened into sinew,
His knuckles white skinned and tissue.
Deboned inane beneath like nightfall,
Cold stone became his teeth and eyeballs.
The sky seemed to fall upon his face,
Sighs of grief called into the ages.
The sky pulled his heart out of his mouth,
It tried to haul it across the clouds.
The sky and water then turned to black,
In time's distorted amnesiac.
In the hours that then followed, lingered,
Tar, the coward, through sorrow drifted.
All the colours of the world vanished,
Withdrew unloved unto his languish.
Through the soil of the woods and hillsides,
Came turmoil underfoot from inside.
A black swamp of thick dead water welled,
And in that want of light - dreaded fell.
Falling into the dark black water,
Gnawing at Tar's dead heart were monsters.
Creatures of such an ancient evil,
Teeth, pure fire, ate at his heels.
They dragged him deeper into abyss,

Stabbing between his breaking ribs.
To beyond the place of fire water,
So prolonged in waste and ire torture.
Below the veil of smoke, rock, and mist,
Into the frail bespoken adrift.
He spiralled down through far voided voids,
Where defiled construed and marred conjoined.
An orgasm of flooded cries aflame,
To a chasm of blood and fire came.
Pain and torment were his only sights,
Rained down torrents of shadow alight.
Through oceans of misery he drowned,
Emotions hideously he found.
Black, if black wasn't something to be,
Lacked; because nothing was it seemed.
No hope, no goodness, no meaning left,
So-groped hooded demons at his chest.
These creatures, formless in their makeup,
Some toothless, clawing in his disrupt.
They had no faces, these bastard beasts,
Their hands were shapeless as dastard teeth.
Escaping never dooming sorrows,
Cascaded deeper tombs of wallow.
As death has face than so too has grief,
In depths, this place, unmasked-so this beast.
Abject pain, contorted all features,
Ashen grains and tortured small creatures.
Nightmare skulls in lonely valleys dwelled,
Somewhere howled bony man of shells.
Burnt trees and hot seas, serpent locusts,
Learnt pleas of mercy went unnoticed.
Mountains collapsed and lakes consumed them,

Hounded elapsed, the take abusive.
The shores of here were bathed in sulphur,
Abhorred the fair who came insofar.
Men's eyes were made of pale and grey rock,
Their crying faded shale laden rot.
Masses crawled up endless horizons,
Darkness stalled their desperate trials.
Women drank from rivers made of sand,
Humans drunk in poison's idle lands.
Birds flew not in the air, but circles,
Forward swam not the fish nor turtles.
Trees grew inside out with leaves of stone,
Breezes blew a bird's feathers into bones.
People drank fire and ate their shadows,
Feeble sang admired fated sorrows.
Severe was this askew defiling,
Unclear crisis, the humans - lifeless.
Carnage, despair, he fell inner-more,
Incarnate leered the spells wicked awe.
Sinking on, the depth untwisting ill,
Drinking from the septic misty hills.
The cold wind blew numbing ice to air,
Old wings knew none suffice to fly here.
Spider webs wrapped around his body,
Binding threads trapped amount embody.
The cobwebs of the ancient spiders,
Around his legs arranging tighter.
Breaking free from the old arachnids,
Making fields of molten acids.
Tree bark made of rock and ember's ash,
The dark ways of shocking tremors crash.
Rotting corpses and dying forests,

Clotting horrid the eyes abolished.
Of these visions, dreadful goats and pigs,
Cause this image, fearful loathsome's dig.
The hurt, though real, had false insane,
Alert survival, Tar's pulsing brain.
"Where am I?" he soon asked of himself,
"With the dying!" booming answer called.
"A field of sadness and grim employ,
You yield its madness, you'll be destroyed."
"Who speaks?" Tar cried, watching the mayhem,
"You, the weak", sighed the voice inside him.
"Am I talking to myself?" he thought,
"Can I walk into mind's ill so-wrought?"
Seeing a cave way in the distance,
A being-unnamed lured insistence.
It had no face, its form was changing,
It embodied gormless rearranging.
In dazed and ghostly affixed horror,
Tar gazed more closely at this monster.
Crawling on hands and knees towards it,
Spawned and disbanded bees and hornets.
Finally reaching the cave's wide mouth,
Violently stinging, the bees flew south.
He looked back to see where they had flown,
A brook, which that turned them back to stones.
And in the cave, he could hear a noise,
Wherein sounded like children's voices.
And in an instant of noise and light,
Tar returned into the Earth upright.
A crying child sought refuge in him,
Its dying idle brought him therein.
Pulled out of his nightmarish vision,

Held onto this child's cherished wishes.
It was only then that he noticed,
He was still holding Saha - lifeless.
The boy who pulled Tar from the nightmare,
Was all too young for all this warfare.
Tar tried to offer him some comfort,
Despite all that which he had suffered.
The evening softened the light from day,
Indeed the hunters at nighttime came.
Their return was met with shock and pain,
Fear did burn regret, they held the slain.
Baha couldn't console anyone,
Chief of them, the eldest of his sons.
Arn's face was white, his hurt beyond scale,
No place left for life, words all did fail.
He stood, motionless, dropping his spear,
Manhood's erosion, allotted fear.
His girls, young and partner, murdered bled,
His world hung in laughter's morbid dead.
Collapsing to his knees, weeping crawl,
Elapsing through seas of feasting's gall.
He sobbed by the bodies of his loves,
Alu and her baby, wondrous once.
Stroking their cooling faces, so soft,
Revoking foolish traces thereof.
Their lot had been quick and quick of end,
His rot to be sick, too sick to mend.
All the other hunters did the same,
As they found their loved ones overcame.
A fresh new wave of dark black water,
As each became apart the slaughter.
The grief seeping from the nearby trees,

Like the thieves sneaking had gone unseen.
The black sky of night fell upon them,
Rollback the tides of fright abhorrence.
Tears and wailing, the hunters so-mourned,
Fearful wading like Tar had before.
He watched as grief took of their spirits,
Recalled no relief of its visit.
Time had ended, or so it would seem,
Children dead and a parent's scream.
The wind fell cold upon their faces,
Its sting took hold of long embraces.
The tears of pain rose from their stomachs,
Despairing rained in frozen torrents.
Sadness, so complete and relentless,
Humans, elite of the tormented.
As the dullness of the pain deepened,
To the culprits, hunters' vengeance.
Lying next to the peaceful bodies,
Crying, "Death to!" - Arn's vengeful plotting.
Other hunters with slaughtered victims,
Too did wonder, "Who butchered them?"
The eyes of the huntsmen turned to Tar,
The lives of their kin burned on his guard.
"Raiders emerged from in the forest,
They slayed the children, clubbed the smallest.
They snatched the women, they took one each,
Unmatched killing ones they didn't need."
Tar finished retelling of events,
Arn in sickness, spewed at the repent.
"You coward must've been one to hide,
For why would they leave the man alive?"
Tar couldn't tell them he was asleep,

This would have to be his shame to keep.
"I would like to help you find these thieves,
We should strike them and make them grieve.
I can fight", Tar said to his brother,
"I desire them so-dead and suffered."
Arn's anger was as blunt as winter,
"You've never been a hunter, brother.
You can't hunt for simple minded beasts,
You're just a feeble, idle weakling.
And you are not my brother", Arn then said,
"If not our father, I'd have you dead.
You have already failed us today,
Few saved from death yet you wail away.
If it were not for our dear parents,
See it now forgot, soured their sparing!"
Arn then turned his back on his brother,
And went to churn in grief another.
In the presence of grief's lingering,
Tar's repentance was chief's figuring.
Baha turned to reason with his sons,
"All have suffered, grieving makes us one."
Was then the boy who sought Tar's comfort,
Told them the story of his slumber.
"He was sleeping!" decried the small youth,
"So their creeping un-spied", came the truth.
Baha paused, glancing to his weak son,
"Is it true?" he asked, "Does he speak some?"
Tar did not answer with spoken words,
And in his silence, served truth occurred.
Anger's fury raged through the hunters,
Slackened duty made them to thunder.
"Kill him!" - "Kill the coward!" - "Murderer!"

"We'll make him pay for our slain daughters!"
Father saved son with fast acting speech,
Baha so-made one last backing plea.
"Enough of death's cold whispers today,
Get up, forget, bold distance away.
You're no longer part of this kinship,
We're much stronger without you in it.
You will always be my boy, my son,
But you can't stay, you destroyed our young.
These men rightly want to have you dead,
Grieving nightly for what's done to them.
I cannot keep you safe anymore,
This is the best outcome of them all.
Be gone, go fend for yourself out there,
Because defend you, I cannot here."
Tears fell from Baha's eyes down his face,
"Go well, my son", cried in drowning ache.
Tar didn't try to plead repentance,
He could only sigh in acceptance.
To vanish but cast no chance to live,
Tar's banishment was Baha's last gift.
Arn didn't acknowledge his brother,
Instead, he chose not to farewell him.
He lay down with Saha and Alu,
And waded round those valleys of gloom.
"Arn, thank-you for looking after me",
And, with that, Tar let his brother be.
Before Tar left, Baha gave him food,
"Forgive me", he wept, "I love you."
"Nothing to forgive", came Tar's reply,
"Owing you, for twice you gave me life."
"Take my spear and this flame", Baha said,

"Take care and someday we'll meet again."
Tar took hold of the flaming torchlight,
Shivered in the cold of coming night.
And he accepted his father's spear,
Full of regret and disparaged fear.
Baha sought to calm his frightened son,
And-so; thought of something wise become.
"The world isn't here to frighten us,
We're here for its showing light and love.
Keep calm, keep still, remember the earth,
No harm can spill from the river's worth."
And with this advice and last embrace,
Tar so-left the campfire's warming ways.
Leaving the camp where he was reviled,
Heaving in shame and into exile.
Into the dark of isolation,
Undo his heart against all creation.
Like the smoke from a fire extinguished,
So was hope he'd survive diminished.
The howls and coos of a moon wild night,
The owl's and hooves, set loose child of fright.
Barking in silhouettes and night mist,
Darkness but for his torch was sightless.
He found a woodland to sleep the night,
Ground was good enough to keep his fire.
Leaves and wind fell to the dust of sleep,
Trees begin telling of trust in dreams.
For days, Tar stumbled about the ground,
He stayed off hunger with fruit he found.
Using his spear as best he knew how,
Masking his fear, he went on the prowl.
The animals won all the battles,

No meals coming from deer nor jackals.
Hunger was Tar's only companion,
Thundered insides, lonely abandon.
Days went by and still he caught nothing,
Slow erasing time, death incoming.
Tree fruit kept him alive, but in weakness,
Astute his eyes, but limbs in meekness.
The wilderness, no place of refuge,
But willingness forsaken deluge.
Taking his father's piece of wisdom,
Made his way to eat of rivers.
Hearing the rushing of a river,
The stirring sounds of life delivered.
Remembering how his father did,
A small dam of rocks for trapping fish.
Days and nights were as lungs drawing breath,
Remained by the riverside on fish.
But fish alone wouldn't keep him fed,
Their flesh and bones couldn't fend off death.
And soon the fish changed their swimming route,
And too the woods lamed in giving fruit.
And-so; he began to waste away,
Into the rhythm of starving's crave.
Tar had not the energy for more,
Nor did he want to go on at all.
But he chose to reflect on beauty,
Flowers growing in absolutely.
For Tar had seen the world of darkness,
Imparted teeming, sad and charmless.
Seeing beyond the pain of it all,
So-choosing the bond in nature's call.
The softness of a gentle sunset,

And often glowing purple subset.
In moments between sleep and slumber,
His torment unseen, deep incumbent.
He remained by the rushing river,
When overcame a sense familiar.
"I have seen this current's way", he thought,
"Have I been to this same place before?"
Here, in some simple moment; a truth,
There greened some apple grown; a fruit.
Unbeknownst to him, a chance happened,
Undergrowth of tree, a plant's apple.
He was lying in a tree's shadow,
Where his mother was buried had grown.
Under fallen leaves and marked with stones,
No doubt, taller apple tree had grown.
Where he had planted the simple seed,
Here had so-started an apple tree.
And in this instant, Tar did-so know,
Planted wisdom of how it had grown.
"The seed! It turned into its parent,
We need to learn how to inherit.
No longer would we need hunt the wild,
Come hunger, could tame seeds, eat the child.
If plants, their breeds, could be so-harnessed,
Disarm all needs upon the harvest.
The hunters would need not risk their blood,
Redundant if we've got fruits and plants."
Agriculture, Tar did envision,
"Is this gesture my late redemption?"
Tar picked an apple off of the tree,
He kissed its natural skin of green.
Biting into its soft nourishment,

Righting hunger with replenishment.
Mothers, human and Earth, saved his life,
Colours, hues, were rebirthed in daylight.
Though he couldn't know this at the time,
So had altered course of human life.
From this humble thought of growing crops,
Tar stumbled on potential unlocked.
Farmers could stay in a single place,
From this would make a settlement named.
Cities would thus emerge and prosper,
Victories thrust to works and culture.
People would wonder and learn and write,
Therefore, their knowledge would then survive.
Art and power and empire glories,
Star gazing towers, mythic stories.
Leaders of tribes would be strong in mind,
Feeders of wives would plough long in kind.
Indeed, the inspiration started,
Seed of civilization planted.
This is where the human world begun,
Because in fear a man couldn't hunt.
Of course, this was all yet to happen,
For Tar was miles from his encampment.
He needed to relocate his clan,
And teach them all, implement his plan.
Farewelling his mother, he set out,
After his brother and father's doubt.
He knew they would need to be convinced,
And hoped that he could be forgiven.

PART III

The Roots

A man of mystery, Bin Ali,
Nomad of history, so he seemed.
Hailing from the great realm of Persia,
Sailing was he with some from further.
On merchant ship, they crossed the ocean,
In surging trip, boat tossed in motion.
Far from the sweet Iranian trees,
Across the deep Arabian Sea.
Their quest begun in Persepolis,
Their rest undone for one sole purpose.
A mathematician by day trade,
To Ali proposition was made.
Rumour had passed through the eastern winds,
To the castle halls of Persian kings.
One such king bid of Ali's presence,
And to a quest should he accept it.
"There is a man", the king contended,
"Wherein he has number invented.
They say his name is Brahmagupta,
They say his fame covers India.
What these numbers are, we do not know,
Could they be witchcraft or reason's own?
Or are these just legends from the east,
Awesome eavesdrops destined to decease?
Go then, Bin Ali, find this guru,
Owe a visit to lands of Hindus.
Make for the port of Barbarikon,

Take an escort the river beyond.
This is where we believe him to be,
In somewhere amidst the jungle trees.
Learn of his ancient wisdoms unknown,
Earn of these secrets and bring them home.
For gifts await your life returning,
So swift about your time to Persia."
The mystery was far too tempting,
To its intrigue, Ali accepted.
And-so; he said farewell to his wife,
Knowing he'd be away for some time.
"Odelia, riches of my heart,
To answer these digits, I depart.
The king requests my skill with numbers,
So I'm sent to fulfil his covets.
The palace will purchase all you need,
To suffice our children while I leave.
Please take good care of our little ones,
Childhood is theirs, our daughters and sons.
And be kind to yourself too, my love,
Do remind yourself of truth above.
But know every moment we're apart,
That you will never stray from my heart.
Your grace of white, my lasting candle,
Your face will light the darkest channels.
When I close my eyes, I will see yours,
When I open them, thy still occurs.
You are in the fabric of myself,
Sewn into my making as thyself.
I can't remember life without you,
I shan't endeavour to ever try to.
Whenever I feel lost or afraid,

I'll remember your closeness portrayed.
If the dark of loneliness takes ye,
Busy yourself with homely makings.
And keep in your heart and memory,
Our weeks apart are temporary.
For I will return, this I promise,
Before Allah's yearning and solace.
I love you, my dear, Odelia,
My isle of truth, whose eyes are sweetest.
For you're warmer than the summer breeze,
In all your form and your woman's ease.
Waterfalls all current to the sea,
One is all and One is you and me."
Though she wept for ache of his going,
Duly accept; save for this knowledge.
"If I die and you're a widower,
Take not bride from over India.
If you come home and find I am dead,
Marry a Persian bride", she said.
Ali took her by her gentle hand,
And he looked her in her tears unplanned.
"Above you, woman, is nothing else,
I love you more than this life itself.
If I return to find death has you,
Sobeit learned, he will have me too."
Embracing, man and wife whole did kiss,
And tracing hands, cried their souls to mist.
At the harbour, Ali chose a ship,
Atlas markers, sailors, came with it.
"A voyage to India?" they asked,
Employ wage of silver paid their task.
So on the seas of the world they set,

Beyond the needs of fishermen's nets.
They crossed the curving of the distance,
To lands serving kings of Indians.
Ferocious waves or a lulling smooth,
The ocean was beautiful and blue.
Ali stood at the bow of the ship,
Where he could feel the blow of the winds.
The nomad of history daydreamed,
About the mysteries stored in waiting.
It seemed to him the rumours untrue,
Conceived it dim some numbers unused.
As they sailed to foreign kingdom gates,
So too the crew spoke, "What numbers wait?"
To ease any superstitiousness,
Ali reassured no wickedness.
"It is likelier there's new colours,
Though this idea contains own wonders.
This fine Hindu mathematician,
Science guru, he's no magician.
So please, fear not, my devoted crew,
With ease buy lots, while I seek guru.
If I return with no newer head,
Buy up, sojourn, and to rumour bed.
With spices, fruit, trinkets, treasures more,
Nicest loots we'll sell at Persia's door.
Sure, fame relies on us ending doubt,
But your families will not miss out."
So they sailed their mathematician,
The blue horizon came in rhythm.
Days and nights sailed under moonlit stars,
With rays of light hailing truth afar.
Only the sky remembers the sea,

And only the sea has memories.
And as each wave is the entire sea,
Universe is the human being.
When came the day, at last, the harbour,
Then made the bay with masts in starboard.
The teeming port of Barbarikon,
A heaving court of markets foreign.
Fishermen and spice trading commerce,
Riches from across the Orient.
The heat, the commotion, human life,
A reprieve from the ocean's deprive.
The ship was moored and crew safely housed,
Equipped with stores, Ali asked around.
"Where do the men of intellect stay?
Their clues adventure send me my way."
"To the town centre", said innkeeper,
"They are proud mentors and truth seekers."
So Bin Ali headed hitherto,
And bid him well said deed from his crew.
Through the streets of bustling commotion,
Produce, receipts, transactions spoken.
Wonders from China and further east,
Vendors of fine arts and treasure chests.
Food, the kind Ali had never seen,
Fruit, his eyes in a mad disbelief.
Spice and grain, calls in market mayhem,
Rice and cane stalls; a naked daydream.
But hunger of a different kind,
Shut mongers out of interest's mind.
For though the wonders were exotic,
None were the numbers Ali wanted.
With that did find in market centre,

Where sat the minds by carpet vendors.
Gathered in debate and conjecture,
Sat the men who conflated lectures.
Paper scrolls; ink-written in Sanskrit,
Pages rolled, hints given in tantric.
Diagrams of the skies and planets,
It was all like some science banquet.
Intrigued the text, Ali studied them,
Mystique and speed, they wrote in hurried pen.
Upon seeing Bin Ali arrive,
Response being, "Member new arise?"
Introducing himself in Persian,
One deduced the tongue so-conversing.
"You've come from far, my friend", said the man,
"But your tongue's comforts end in these lands."
"Perhaps you may help me?" Ali asked,
"Translate, convey my difficult task?"
"Of your task, say it then", said the man,
"Offer it masked phrases when I can."
"I am seeking Brahmagupta's home,
I've been sent here by my kingdom's throne.
A fare I'll pay to be shown his face,
Is there any here who know his place?"
The man translated Ali's request,
Began speculation for their guest.
Ali listened to their coloured speech,
And he wished to hear a word of each.
"They think he's some weeks up the river,
Beware, seldom speaks to visitors.
The river too is lined with danger,
Deliver you though it will, stranger.
At the harbour you can rent a boat,

Pay a wager for the river go."
"Thank-you, graciously", Ali replied,
"To pursue maths maharishi's mind."
Back through the town to the river's mouth,
A crew of scouts, Ali called them out.
"I have seven silver Persian coins,
For brave endeavour-me a voyage.
I seek a journey, far the river,
I need a tour to Brahmagupta."
Only one scout accepted Ali,
"Sir, without my trek you can't succeed."
He was cocky with youth's confidence,
But Ali sought some reassurance.
"Is that so?" Bin Ali asked the scout,
"It is known", he replied, "There's no doubt.
Not one scout here speaks a word you do,
I recount pieces of Persian's muse.
Without me, you will die up river,
I'll scout you to your Brahmagupta."
"Then let us go upstream together,
Your debt thus paid in gleaming silver."
"My price is twenty Persian pieces,
Is your life worthy of expenses?"
"Fifteen and settled", Ali proposed,
"This seems a better deal", scout supposed.
And-so; with stocks and arming with swords,
Their boat undocked with them both aboard.
Paddling to the river's open mouth,
Battling delta's waters flowing south.
The river's water soon slowed to ease,
The city's walls exchanged jungle trees.
To Ali, the jungle seemed gorgeous,

He'd never seen such green of fauna.
The richness of the magic nature,
Saw witness fauna's drastic strangeness.
Heat and insects clogged the afternoon,
Of trees and sweat, long in the pursuit.
At sunset's hour, both men were worn out,
Riverbank; a fire, Ali and scout.
Cooking dinner, they spoke of loved ones,
Women, liquor, their daughters and sons.
Ali's thoughts drifted into Persia,
To his daughters and sons of nurture.
He saw his wife's soft face in his mind,
In her white-washed grace and hazel eyes.
With long black hair over her shoulders,
No wrong actions in her composures.
What it was to know of love like hers,
Pitied he did brothers nothing learned.
And-so; miles from home, he slept this night,
Though awhile bemoaned and dreamt of wife.
But for all his love of her graces,
The call to search for divine's traces.
There was more to seem than man of ease,
Fearful calls to peer discoveries.
As the fire reduced to embers,
Ali's desires so-switched to numbers.
"To find something new is a man's goal,
Remind touching then can woman's soul.
Is it really figures I've come for,
Cities, theories, mysteries, numbers?
Or does this quest have deeper meaning,
Orders behest to seek redeeming?
Mathematics; the language of stars,

Charismatic, the vanquish of Mars.
Geometries and Greek Socrates,
Anomalies of sleek qualities.
The Universe is rich of beauty,
I do observe its tricks, oft mutely.
True face of God might soon await me,
Illusion's gone and looms abating."
Prior frets swooned under the numbers,
Tiredness soon took Ali's slumber.
Come the morning, scout and Ali woke,
Sun up early, rounded into boat.
Forging upstream, heat and danger more,
Scorching sunbeams meeting ranger's oars.
Vines, fauna, and humid jungle air,
Warmed dangerous human fungal-snare.
For eight days straight, they journeyed upstream,
And late came ways of horrid disease.
Both scout and Ali, soon sickness fell,
Host and hunger weakened vicious ills.
But silver wage and Sultan orders,
Kept still their voyage, tainted waters.
Then came day nine of their fated trip,
Unfazed, they ventured, furthered sickness.
Till came a waterfall descending,
"We'll walk jungle floor", scout suggesting.
Carrying canoe above their heads,
Navigating wild amuck they led.
But disaster hit the explorers,
When their raft slipped on down the waters.
And with it went Ali's abacus,
Downstream also sent his papyrus.
All his calculations swept away,

Years of dedication, wrecked dismay.
No gold could ever replace reward,
His sole possession was now his sword.
"Good sir, we must return to harbour,
Procure new raft, discern new charter."
"Going back will kill me", Ali yearned,
Knowing he was too ill to return.
The scout already feared death's grip,
And he doubted he'd survive the trip.
"I can't reach this number man on foot,
He can't teach us if we can't endure.
Your money, sir, I'll leave with your men,
All the silver coins, fifteen of them.
A month to hike to the temple steps,
I hope you find Bengal's number prince."
"Farewell", Ali wished his trusty scout,
"Please tell my crew I still seek about.
But you must keep all the silver coins,
Here is fifteen more for your employ.
This quest was strange and somewhat token,
Unrest and danger to go with it.
But you gave me a fine reminder,
That truth mostly resides inside us.
To your Barbarikon family,
Go journey well, my young companion."
The men parted ways with a handshake,
Then separate made each their pathways.
And-so; Ali forged ahead himself,
Alone and sick, urged again impelled.
Days and days, Ali hiked the jungle,
Chased by fever, escaped and stumbled.
Nature, the kind not found in Persia,

Danger remained unbound in Asia.
There came moments of rest's reflection,
Unnamed creatures and beast impressions.
Monkeys swung from vines and in the trees,
This was a countryside only dreamed.
Parrots of vibrant coloured feathers,
With chorus sounds of fragrant treasures.
Ancient insects of ruthless design,
Waiting unslept with their toothless bite.
The days were long and of choking heat,
Like waves of strong, restless, smoking sleep.
The golden sunlight of India,
Unwoven each night to blackened air.
Then the jungle's heat gave into warmth,
Only until each morning's return.
Along the riverside, Ali kept,
Hiking in the daylight, fire slept.
Eating fish and jungle fruit he found,
Heaving sick in the unwell surrounds.
But the mystery of the numbers,
Curious mystique kept him fumbling.
Driven by white unwavering lust,
Enlist the right man, had king entrust.
Mere explorers would've not sufficed,
Fear of not knowing is what survived.
In the moments when all hope felt lost,
The numbers kept Ali's forfeit crossed.
As days wore on in this dense jungle,
A pledge swore upon his six children.
"Should sooner die than not uncover,
Would ruin my mind, rot in wonder.
My children would be ashamed of me,

For I willed my own insanity.
And to my wife, I'd be no husband,
No peace of mind, forever numbers.
The nagging of this uncertainty,
A jagged truth curiosity.
Therefore I must find Brahmagupta,
And eye his writing proof of rumour.
And if this man has spread lies abroad,
Sobeit his red will dye my sword."
Punishing heat, unrelenting sun,
Menacing feet, fermented mud.
Intense the heat and begun to see,
Invented head - hallucinating.
So sure he had reached the digit raj,
But lured instead of mistress mirage.
Where Ali envisioned a temple,
There it had been positioned mental.
Salt-sweat, delirium soon set in,
All wet, bacteria brewed within.
His vision blurred and throat ached in thirst,
And his skin burned, torso draped in curse.
So weak he became with each step made,
That went unseen that a tiger preyed.
The orange and black stalked in silence,
It followed his track, walked beside him.
And when it leapt, so swift and deadly,
Its whitened teeth bit into Ali.
The blood and screams and the tiger's roar,
Red flooded limbs and the fighter's gore.
Swiping paws fretted in the attack,
As the claws shredded across his back.
And in his mind, Ali saw his wife,

"You don't want to die, you have to fight!"
Instinct of man, alert survivor,
Instant his hand for sword incisor.
Ali grabbed his metal rapier,
And he stabbed it in the tiger.
Its fur went from orange to crimson,
Its hurt sent it roaring in frenzy.
Wrestling pain and fear in noble dance,
Destined either slain, revered their chance.
Bud of flower in the muddied sand,
Blood of tiger and bloodied of man.
No evil design, nabbing man of sword,
But regal feline was stabbed three times more.
And when the animal stopped to die,
Ali impartial comforted lie.
He stroked its reddened fur with his hand,
Unspoken respect for death and damn.
Almost more than the bond of lovers,
Foremost war and beyond all others.
But prey won victory at high cost,
And lay down jittery in blood lost.
The Persian mathematician lay,
In hurting and unforgiving pain.
As his blood flowed in severe amounts,
Handed to unknown, he then blacked out...
Conscious scent, breathed silk, thin banded air,
Softness, gentle, sweet milk's skin and hair.
Women whisper sunlight, something there,
Bosom, drifting one night, blushing care.
Becoming, humming, gasp the lungs and eyes,
The touching, drumming, clasp the young disguise.
Light does flutter, seen by being's skin,

Life is but a dream by dreaming things.
Blinked - lashes; the face, your face or mine,
Slinked, flashes of age, persuade of thine.
Years, days; our time is short, shorter still,
Fears, ways; sour vines distort trauma's will.
Between raspy breaths, the waking few,
Recede thusly the depths, aching through.
Back to black, black to black and black awe,
That too, retract, to that retracts more...
Ali woke, but knew nothing of else,
So he spoke, "What's new, so bring of help?"
Then to his ears, so sweet, came a voice,
Into his tears this sleet calm rejoice.
Spoken in her mother's tongue and hers,
Broken in verse, colour sung in words.
A woman, beautiful in essence,
None could tune a mute sound so precious.
Time had passed, though the sands were unknown,
Tiger's last; owed his hands to her bones.
Golden bracelets flowed from this mistress,
In a graceful moment of stillness.
In her soft face, shaped of envy's lust,
With myrrh embrace, draped in jewels and dust.
Like a white bird in the black of space,
Life so-unlearned how to know such grace.
Green silk against her black hair, her lips,
Her frame; accentuate heartbreak's gift.
Her eyes, pale brown, the deepest windows,
Sunrise a gown; entreat this Indo.
Therein had desire's dwell of her curl,
The instant his eyes fell on this girl.
The spell of love, or lust, or beauty,

Cast well some to last untruthfully.
A wife in Persia, loyal in ache,
She cried in fervour, embroiled wait.
Casting his heart to Persepolis,
Lasting depart from her lasting kiss.
There she stood, in white pillars of stone,
Leered and hooded, wife figure alone.
His heart broke at the sighs or her face,
His arms choked at the sides of her waist.
The longing, the hurt, human the pain,
Belonging to her movement the same.
"To hurt-so is to be of this life",
He thought-so, "Lest to be is to die."
Yearning for want of a better man,
Unlearned adultery, never than.
He wanted to be a child again,
And chance to reconcile this pain.
Such a thing in maths was so affine,
Much nothing alas translates in life.
Parallel partnerships permitted,
Infidel numbered sins committed.
Regret and worry soon enveloped,
Panic and eerie loom embellish.
Ali called for his wife, his sweetheart,
She enthrall ignored his plight's remark.
The Indian girl knelt in closeness,
And whispering some, dealt him dotage.
Her worried frown on her darkened skin,
She wondered how converse-speak to him.
From the colour of their skin and words,
Wondered other, inferred them unheard.
Understanding her words were not known,

She showed him the bandages she'd sewn.
With gentle hand, she took his in hers,
In careful scan, he shook with the hurt.
Ali was in righteous agony,
And he tossed in crisis casualty.
This angel's name, if known, could aid him,
Its meaning came 'scholar' - Adhita.
She offered him a pipe to smoke on,
Of copper rim, pain bribed him toke some.
A rich assail his bloodied making,
To which inhale, his body aching.
Breathing out the herb marijuana,
Sheathing hurt, usurped by Mama.
Unto the pale waterfall of wine,
And through the veil of all life and time.
Under the sweep of sixty shadows,
Unto the sleep of misty meadows...
The gift of life returned to Ali,
His drifting mind concerning body.
Though pain was less than it was before,
Abstain confess; spirit lusted more.
Adhita, her eyes weary from time,
Was seated inside her home reside.
Cooking on a stove and fire's coal,
Wooden home alcove, she perspired toll.
His eyes and heart cheated on his wife,
This wise desire met with inner strife.
"Forgive a nuptial moment of sway,
It is natural to feel this way.
You nearly died and she saved your bones,
So clearly why you feel payment owed.
Do not confuse debt for lover's just,

Forgot refuse tempt of other's lust."
That said - a reeling passionate ensued,
In red feeling, fashioned the prelude.
Instinct lured him to take her body,
"Give thanks for curing, make her folly."
Adhita brought him a meal and milk,
And he did caution conceal his will.
"Eat and pay her silver", he reasoned,
"And same way, she prefers you leaving."
Though it hurt to do, he ate his meal,
Knew the worth of food, that gracious feel.
But when Ali went to rise and leave,
Was then he was bent in pain's retrieve.
She rushed to guide him back to his bed,
And hushed subside, lilac fuming rest.
Days and nights of this routine passed by,
Pains and sighs, a slow decrease of thine.
In their time together in her home,
Confide some to gather facts so-known.
Adhita's husband had died years been,
So she was cast, damned aside unseen.
Her only child, a girl, taken far,
In lonely wild, she toiled, broken heart.
Ali tried to share his equations,
But he failed in bare explanations.
Able though to relay of his spouse,
Ali chose to indicate without.
A howling crime, divine vow forsakes,
A thousand times his wife's heart would break.
Odelia's memory abandoned,
Hideous treachery imagined.
Nonetheless, she nursed him, devoted,

Some success from worsened heroics.
And all the while, Ali kept his oath,
Even at times when she was unclothed.
Until he was well enough to leave,
Stood still, she was selling self naive.
More now to wait or come the warm rush,
For how she ached for a man's firm touch.
Ali's leaving soul was tearing so,
Would he cheat his own or dare to go?
"How can I love more than one woman,
And hand to them all the same owing?
Quran sayeth so my dilemma;
'Even if it's your ardent desire'.
Allah knows, 'Ye are ever timid,
To be fair and just between women'.
I journeyed to find some new figures,
But searching reminds me old wisdoms.
Any Brahmagupta equation,
Know thee, must not forget, verbatim.
One is the great truth, my Lord and wife,
Wonder abates youth, no flaws derive."
So to Adhita's sweet doleful eyes,
Ali had to retreat hopeful guise.
The wicked cruelty of the Devil,
To widowed jewel for use as vessel.
Kissing her hand and kneeling before,
Missing a man, she fell lower more.
Eye to eye, they saw in each other,
That they might die, beseeched them lovers.
Imploring human hearts of satin,
The soaring truth imparts this pattern.
That love and fear cannot be numbered,

And that's why their onslaught is hungered.
That the dreaming things know they're nothing,
But fear, it seems, does sing them something.
Knowledge and love, blinded each their souls,
Bonded at once in life's sweet condole.
That they are but small and tender babes,
Even passed their crawl to their sailing ways.
Imperfect and frightened, they need care,
A verdict, suffice it some aware.
It was just a kiss to reassure,
Life is thus and it's to be adored.
A moment of scent's warmest feelings,
Remembered them they're human beings.
It was a moment she'd longed for so,
And there was no omen-wrong unrobed.
Just a hint for her to remember,
Where love is and is never hindered.
Stay she now in this blissful lasting,
And Ali vowed no listless parting.
They parted ways, in honour of both,
Their hearts had stayed, no words were spoken.
Returning to the jungle's green heat,
Sunburn and vines tangled indiscreet.
Hiking back towards the river's edge,
Striking track on water's ridge ahead.
Full of life - reborn - he filed upstream,
Dullest miles no more, now wildest dreams.
The beauty of the world amazed him,
"It's truly worth unequalled praising."
The smells enchanting touch and the light,
He felt like dancing, such was his high.
He carried on upstream, day and night,

Through valleys, jungle leaves, and life.
Then, just four days up the current's rush,
There laid bare a patch that wasn't lush.
He spied in the jungle canopy,
The spire of a temple in the trees.
Tricked once already by that mistress,
Blinked twice to steady this as witness.
The red stonework didn't fade away,
Instead frozen in the light of day.
In his chest, his heart began to race,
So behest a start to runner's pace.
The stonework was draped in vines and green,
Twisting circles shaped the spire he'd seen.
Into the shade grand maths cathedral,
Became afraid at the lack of people.
"Ruined this place where once wonders host,
Am I too late, are the numbers ghost?"
The sun shined warm in the empty halls,
The jungle vines climbed upon the walls.
"Here stands the place, but none here remain,
A grand palace of numbers contain.
Carvings etched onto edifices,
Markings stretch but who accredited?"
Secrets displayed all around Ali,
Genius arranged, foreign the writing.
The mystery numbers were right there,
But inquiry of them; thousand years.
Ali cursed his fate for being so,
And outburst his lateness screaming, "No!"
Was then he heard a sound somewhere near,
And the Persian soon found out from where.
With slow tapping of his walking stick,

Brahmagupta arrived, talking quick.
"Who comes to my school with sword to shout?
No sums, and why Persian word of doubt?"
Ali knew who this old man must be,
Lowered his sword and told hastily.
"Good sir, my relief you are alive,
Infer my belief you'd not survived.
I have travelled for many a month,
Luck unravelled in search of your sums.
Rumour has reached the kings of Persia,
New numbers preach, you are inventor.
Across an ocean, up that river,
A quest I've known, sir Brahmagupta.
From Persepolis, I seek knowledge,
Your eloquence, please teach me of it."
Brahmagupta studied long his guest,
Ali offered money, silver's best.
"These numbers ended my academy,
Conquerors alleged my blasphemy.
They came with fire and they destroyed all,
Just fame and ire lie behind these walls.
So keep your silver, my Persian friend,
Indeed you'll need it down river's bend."
Ali refused to just quit so fast,
"Numbers new, does use exist?" he asked.
"Indeed", came Brahmagupta's reply,
"Tell me", came Ali's desperate vie.
Brahmagupta saw Ali's hunger,
"Come with me, I'll show you the numbers."
Old mathematician led the young,
Manifold expedition become.
Through silent halls of stone temptation,

Grew momentous anticipation.
Coming to a darkened passageway,
Clashing swords had marked with ricochets.
A beam of sunlight shone down one end,
It streamed in from slight stone crack ahead.
"Here the numbers sit, my Persian friend,
Where the sunbeam hits them at the end."
Ali trembled and walked down the hall,
To the symbols unlocked on the wall.
His heart beat quickly, his breath shaking,
In the presence of something sacred.
Peering closer through the dusty air,
There in stone read the new digit pair.
"The number on the left", spoke guru,
"I stumbled on its debt hoax value.
It gives weight to nothing, no hero,
It gives shape to something called Zero.
The number on the right intrigues me,
It trusts upon the mind eternity.
To me it is femininity,
It seems call to men Infinity.
There is none so new, my Persian friend,
Values for truth used given instead.
To know; there's only three true numbers,
Zero, Infinity, the wonders.
The third number is not a secret,
In birth, One comes to host albeit.
As two lovers will each discover,
They who number One in each other.
These root numbers are the Universe,
Their fruit grows in gardens we observe.
They all have the same value to me,

We call them love and hate and to be.
The Universe is us, we are it,
This truth resides in life's precious gift.
Universe tries become so equal,
Known truth lies in the love of people."
A tear of joy fell down Ali's face,
For where the void was now love replaced.

PART IV

The Synthesis

The world of man lay in ashen waste,
So-ruined the land, in barren's bathe.
Into howling winds of sand and snow,
Withdrew clouds abandoned lands unknown.
A world of smouldering frozen clay,
Which swirled in cold furnace open flames.
Charred and gaunt, like a starving demon,
Scarred, distraught, light apart from being.
No colour was left in this dead world,
Snow covered in ash and mist demurred.
Everything had been ripped of colour,
Colouring nondescript from other.
Dead trees stood like ghosts of skeletons,
No leaves, wood-white posts irrelevant.
The skies were dead, overcast and black,
Sunrise unsaid since the blast attack.
Nuclear winter without a spring,
Gloomier winds arrived for nothing.
Deep grey skies hung lower each new day,
Sweeping writhed in smoke and sieged decay.
Days were cold, days were night, nighttime more,
Grey scale and terrified midnight all.
The air was now a toxic sulphur,
Its fair endow had lost its offer.
The oceans blackened in lifeless tides,
A potion acid of typhus mire.
The forests had all burned down aflame,

Their orange delight horned bright insane.
Their smoke rose and blotted out the Sun,
It cloaked below, rotted everyone.
In this tyrant ghoul of windy works,
Deathly silence ruled the blinded Earth.
Humanity dead and it defiled,
Vanity let out the Auschwitz-Howl.
The animals were dead or frightened,
Made cynical unrest or lifeless.
What man had made of fellow beings,
With hands of shade and hollow meaning.
So-hooked on ego's fearful disguise,
To look at God and tear out It's eyes.
In the wake of man's late achievement,
Deadened lakes and betrayed bereavement.
If only the skeletons could scream,
Of lonely embellishment obscene.
Some redemption for man could happen,
Condemnation instead had trapped them.
Morose, evil, extinct, and finished,
Near-most the people were extinguished.
With no saviours left and none to save,
The humans indebt repugnant slaves.
The few who remained lived underground,
Their strewn decay so clearly profound.
The generation responsible,
Their abdication phenomenal.
Their population had plummeted,
From eight billion to just ten thousand.
It was now their great-grandchildren's fate,
To grovel, mutate, and disarray.
They huddled in darkness deep below,

In cuddled partner's weeping sorrow.
Mineshafts; they lived like Iblis roaches,
Bone paths and conditions atrocious.
At least, it could be said, they knew not,
The feast that had been misled their lot.
For know nothing of the world before,
And-so; something of its bliss ignored.
If on the surface they were to live,
Then they'd have clues - alas; none of it.
They might have remembered New Orleans,
Paris or Dublin or Tel Aviv.
They might have known of antiquity,
Egypt or Rome or Hercules.
They might have met the Mona Lisa,
And then beget to know her painter.
They might have heard of Beethoven's Ninth,
Moonlight Sonata or Shakespeare's lines.
They might have found the great CERN circle,
And wondered how the particles twirled.
They might have seen the Burj Khalifa,
The height it reached and yearned achievement.
They might have felt some of Nirvana,
Enlightenment come into flower.
They might have glimpsed pages of books,
Inspired by how the ages once looked.
They might have seen the natural world,
Birds of flight and ease before the hurl.
But they did not, they stayed underground,
And became forgot ways to astound.
Whispers, legends, and myths were spoken,
How this ended and gifted broken.
There was talk of a great worldly state,

Theories so-thought of its late debate.
"They wanted to make one government,
The whole world create dumb parliament.
Where wealthy alone could enjoy it,
Us filthy drones would be exploited.
Their plan took decades to realise,
A planet indebted and chastised.
Their want was violently pursued,
Stormfront and potent weaponry used.
They waged war in every theatre,
Like ageless whores until we feared them.
They battled for people's hearts and minds,
And strangled our love of humankind.
Sophisticated propaganda,
Psychopathic extravaganza.
Divided and conquered, the old trick,
Contrived dishonour to hold us sick.
Division's art gave power to kings,
Religions, classes, even our skins.
They amplified our differences,
And acted like they mattered to us.
Perpetual states of emergency,
And fearful days of urgency.
Until enough people believed them,
That not all their brothers were equal.
People died for their flags and countries,
Evil lies; coloured rags and money.
Consume, consume, consume, and consume,
Immune to doom - the human excuse.
Successful they were, this evil core,
Until a resistant rebel war.
Some people had won their spirits back,

From evil back to the fearless track.
They remembered the light we once held,
That we once helped the life of the world.
They remembered the greed of control,
And endeavoured to seed the revolt.
So they tried to bring about the change,
In a fight for our place so-regained.
But the World Entente was far too strong,
Its torturous want only prolonged.
But in all their strength and years of crime,
The Entente could not prevent demise.
There is a relentlessness to time,
Which causes everything to subside.
The rebel numbers fell to hundreds,
Against twelve million Entente soldiers.
So an unthinkable plan was made,
But to some unspeakable its fate.
The rebels debated with themselves,
The ones unpersuaded soon compelled.
The rebels decided an attack,
Where missiles fired in covert act.
'Better to die than let Empire reign,
Together we'll get hydrogen rain.
It's simply an extinction event,
History has given its consent.
The world will heal in some million years,
And be free of our evil ensnares.
Sorry to life, we have failed you so,
Know that we tried to save your unknown.
If we can't be free, we cannot be,
Rivers aren't for dams and nor are we'.
And-so; rained the hydrogen bombing,

And-so; came no hope of surviving.
Virtually all life was wiped out,
Hurt were the leaves, the animal shouts.
Astronauts had watched from space stations,
As our world was hot-erased in flames.
So did the colonists on the Moon,
Know then the cold witness to their doom.
Like measles on some sickly infant,
Orange flames wiped out city districts.
A black cloud of smoke covered Earth's skies,
It wrapped around, all choked till they died.
Fragments of civilisation left,
Fractured and crippled, starvation swept.
Government did try to reconvene,
And even fixed some broken machines.
But standing armies couldn't survive,
Starving society's endless night.
Chaos spread through whatever remained,
Horrors and death, it all seemed inane.
Institutions crumbled and scattered,
Destitute humans died and scavenged.
Violent gangs took city ruins,
Nihilist acts shook pity's doing.
But they would pay for their violence,
For they would die in this environment.
Under the surface gave only home,
Plunder like worms did; we lowly roam."
This was the lead thought of history,
How came the deed wrought atrocity.
But others refused, called them liars,
Such was the confusion of survivors.
Others questioned the Earth was to blame,

"Mother ended her own scourge-insane.
Humans abused the Earth to extremes,
Hubris refused to move or redeem.
So climate of fate killed human lore,
Primate still own provocateur."
The debate soon did change, however,
"Maybe it's best hid altogether?
Perhaps, to protect our children's minds,
We act as if the world is the mines?
'There is no such thing as the surface,
And even if there is - it's worthless'.
To keep them repressed in these hell holes,
This is the lesser of the evils.
We're in tatters, farmers without crops,
It matters not if the bombs were dropped."
So, deep underground, some humans lived,
To teach ignorant children these fibs.
Some decades of this behaviour passed,
Uneducated until the last.
But the surface radiation fell,
Down the mineshafts and into their health.
People were sick, rotting of cancers,
No medicines, doctors, nor answers.
Along with their drop into the mines,
Growing of crops had been cast aside.
No plants could live in these conditions,
Charmless viruses only permitted.
The stockpiles of food were protected,
But while consumed, they were infected.
And when all of the food had rotted,
All decency was soon forgotten.
A final horror befell people,

A reprisal of a mortal evil.
Humanism left their hearts and their minds,
Cannibalism crept into the mines.
Those who refused to eat flesh soon died,
And those who consumed their meat survived.
But even this would not be enough,
The supply of dead could never last.
And even if there were enough dead,
Humans need more than mere sustenance.
For humans need hope to stay alive,
And losing it, one girl left the mines...
Her name was Rose, she was sixteen years,
Her mine had chosen to abstain theirs.
They never ate of their human dead,
But ever closer they came to it.
And-so; Rose formulated a plan,
To go premeditated upland.
She had heard whispers of a surface,
Overheard secrets spoke in verses.
Little rhymes said in darkened corners,
That the mine hid them from a surface.
Rose was taught to never repeat them,
For her own good to keep them secret.
The mere utterance of these lyrics,
Brought fear's muttering to hysterics.
For most, these rhymes simply gave them chills,
Adults hushed silence, ingrained, instilled.
And though she tried to forget these rhymes,
Rose couldn't drive them from her mind.
Ever in the corners of her eyes,
Were the suspicions about the mine.
And in her teens, Rose came upon proof,

That the mine's machines were gross untruths.
She got lost one day deep in the mine,
But along the way, a secret find.
Covered in soot, she almost missed it,
A nature book engrossed with pictures.
Photographs of trees and animals,
A moments release so magical.
For years Rose kept the book a secret,
And daren't to glance the pages frequent.
But whenever she did she felt free,
In the pleasure of her waking dreams.
So when the famine slowly worsened,
Rose determined to go out searching.
Having spent her childhood in the mine,
Leaving it proved difficult in time.
While her parents were asleep in bed,
She farewelled them, weeping in lament.
"And though it seems like I've abandoned,
Not so, I'll be back with companions.
I'll save you all from this dreadful mine,
You can't live here anymore than I."
Taking her time for some repentance,
She made her way to the mine's exit.
The most complete of forbidden rhymes,
Led Rose's feet to the hidden climb.
"To escape these lies and this madness,
You must take the mine's hidden ladders.
You will not find them on any map,
Because this mine is indeed a trap.
Take level sixty's drift to the bend,
Retracing fifty steps at the end.
Take the third heading's crosscut entry,

To the burnt-out airlock's assembly.
Take the dragline's manway transferring,
Fake is the mainline ways returning.
Then sneak through the unfused barricaded,
Reaching a disused elevator.
The elevator has no power,
But a ladder goes up the tower.
Climb until you see a blinding light,
Light so unlike the electric kind.
In this light, you'll see the real Earth,
Escape this mine and you'll be rebirthed."
With torchlight, Rose scanned the tunnel up,
Soaring heights, it vanished into dark.
She climbed and climbed her way out the ground,
Slow rungs and grime, she daren't look down.
The echoes of her every footstep,
The gallows of her family's depths.
If she fell, she'd fall for miles and scream,
Back to hell and all its while demeaned.
The climb dragged on, her legs grew weaker,
The mine's lagging, begging to keep her.
For hours she clung and continued her climb,
Thousands of rungs until she saw light.
A tiny bit of light miles above,
The tunnel brightening as she climbed.
And at the top she couldn't describe,
Understand what she saw with her eyes.
She had never seen an open space,
Not even one so closed in greys.
The world's intense and striking beauty,
It all brought tears to her eyes to see.
However, her wonder soon gave way,

The weather was not as blue as day.
A coating of grey and ash embalmed,
The smoking remains that had become.
Where was the green in the pages seen,
Where were the creatures of ageless dreams?
Aghast her book could've lied as well,
At last she understood mineshafts dwell.
The world was rage, dark skies inhuman,
Her skin was pale white, like porcelain.
Too cold this wind in the open space,
Took hold her skin, broke upon her face.
With desolate skies and crying winds,
"Return to the mine?" she came to think.
"No! There is nothing of hope down there,
Only the coming threat and despair.
Out here, it's likely I'll meet with death,
But there's nothing surer in the depths.
There's a life worth living, you know it,
Not in mines, but Earth's giving glowing.
Try find one of these so-called cities,
Lined with trees or some new beginnings."
So Rose bravely left the mine behind,
And chose daily theft to try survive.
Into the post-apocalyptic,
Entered this Rose, unspoken, gifted.
The ashen winds kept her moving on,
Its blackened sting left no soothing calm.
Dead and famished cinder abstractions,
Breath of vanished ember extractions.
This was the narcissistic shadow,
That caused the Mars addicted echo.
She walked through emaciated fields,

Undifferentiated surreal.
Things burned, things crumbled, things were not things,
Winds churned, limbs buckled, stinging her skin.
In this lifeless world she wandered lost,
As if silent banshees wanted not.
Until she spied some distant pathway,
Downhill did lie a westward highway.
Reaching the highway, Rose followed it,
Astounding array of hollowed things.
The outer boneyard of a city,
Smoking graveyards of society.
Mangled cars and trucks and skeletons,
Vandal fires destruct American.
Power lines slung on melted street lamps,
Outlined and clung defeated badlands.
Telephone wires laced the blackened sky,
Torrents of fires encased maddened sights.
Rose's first night set in afternoon,
Low was the light in Earth's scattered gloom.
She knew no concept of day or night,
So grew distressed at this end of light.
Afraid, confused, and near scared to death,
She made good use of fear's impetus.
In howling winds, the cold bit her so,
She prowled around for old shelter's home.
Underneath a crumbled overpass,
Of concrete busted nuclear blast.
In broken pillars and her fatigue,
She looked for somewhere to rest her feet.
Sleeping in amongst these ruined stones,
She dreamed of distrusting food alone.

Hunger ate her subconscious mind,
And her stomach rumbled in its grind.
But in the night came proof of legend,
Furious cries, gangs of ruthless men.
Rose awoke and hid with instinct's haste,
Her breath was slow but her heart did race.
But they went on their murderous ways,
In hell-bent rage and permanent hate.
Too bent in stress to lie unafraid,
She spent the rest of the night awake.
The air was laced with hot ashen sleet,
Each breath inhaled it and coughing heat.
The thought crept back inside Rose's head,
"You ought backtrack to the mine instead."
Then in time's slow march came morning's rise,
Wherein skies still dark but dimming light.
So she chose to continue onwards,
Though unknown the potential horrors.
Back on the long dead highway she went,
As blackened fog and skies descended.
The days were now so painfully short,
So made allowed replacement distort.
The second night on her journey west,
In shelter's side to finally rest.
At first light, she awoke in hunger,
And despite it, she kept to wander.
She had very little water left,
But would weary first to hunger's theft.
There was nothing to eat anywhere,
Only the things of sleet and vile air.
Then in the distance, she saw a sign,
With her vision burning ashen eyes.

And as she drew nearer, she could read,
That the letters spelled 'Los Angeles'.
The first forbidden rhyme ever learnt,
Had Los Angeles' name spoke in verse.
"Near the city of Los Angeles,
There lives the last societies."
Underneath the city's name were miles,
Seventeen to reach it pacing while.
Though her stomach groaned in crippling ache,
She followed the road til nightfall came.
She fell asleep in ruins that night,
Wondered what Los Angeles was like.
She hoped she might also come to find,
Someone alike with an honest mind.
Someone with food and water to drink,
Someone who viewed the world like she did.
Someone who wasn't a bandit crook,
Someone who could understand her book.
On this long Californian highway,
She walked along next morning's landscape.
Until a wonder so scandalous,
Crumbled plunder of Los Angeles.
Fire and black, orange and smog decay,
Here was that which Rose had longed to stray.
There was no society in sight,
This was the third great lie of her life.
Chimney ruins and clogged sky buildings,
A city of gulag high workings.
Industrial corpse of concrete land,
Terrestrial warped secreted bland.
Black spires half-ruined and rusting smoke,
Shack fires, pollutant, disgusting cokes.

Man's buildings rotten, seeped with horror,
The devils got what seemed their honour.
The west incineration's doing,
This edge of civilisation's ruin.
The sight of the city made her cry,
"Why? Why did they think it time to die?"
All hope was lost, she surrendered it,
Her only want was a peaceful death.
Looking for a place to starve to death,
She pulled herself with each half footstep.
Down broken roads and black streets of woe,
Town's smoking bones lacking peace for Rose.
So close to the everlasting sleep,
Almost fainting in darkened streets.
And then, when all seemed about to end,
Something amazing allowed instead.
Rose came upon an eerie ruin,
So made bygone library burning.
Built of stone, it was made black from smoke,
In it, though, did remain pages wrote.
She gasped in awe upon her entrance,
For she saw something unimagined.
Thousands of books in hundreds of rows,
Mountains of riches bundled for Rose.
The world had died, she was to follow,
But first she could fly out of shadows.
She found some pages of coloured life,
Astounding natures once so bright.
All the artwork of a poet's pen,
To her observed and the unknown went.
She was wary of violence and harm,
The library was silent and calm.

And for a fragile moment of bliss,
Rose was able to escape in this.
Down a forest path and by a brook,
Sounds of purist song, all from her books.
"So", she thought, "Here I can die in peace",
This sweet daughter found her forest trees...
Some hours went by before Rose awoke,
Came by then her horror - voices spoke!
Moving swiftly, her heart raced in beat,
Hiding quickly, the gang heard her feet.
"Who goes there?" said one, flashing their torch,
And as Rose hid, they actioned towards.
Rose's pulse raced faster and faster,
As they closed in, their lights in casting.
Hiding in ruins of books and stone,
She closed her eyes and hoped they would go.
For dying of hunger was one thing,
But lying in murder appalling.
But they closed in, cornered, surrounded,
And to Rose's horror they found her.
She was blinded by their bright torches,
But decided to fight remorseless.
Too weak, however, were her young bones,
Defeated in a few lunges thrown.
"Be calm!" said a voice, "We won't hurt you,
No harm from us, gentle our virtue."
Rose looked at the gang, bandits of none,
With books in their hands, candid and calm.
"Who are you?" Rose asked with trembling nerves,
"Which violent masked gang do you serve?"
A woman stepped forward and answered,
Rose listened and frowned, still untrusting.

"We serve no gang, we are scientists,
We search the land, seek enlightenment.
We are trying to rebuild the world,
And the lifeblood of it; written words.
And what is your story, my dear girl,
Where did you come from in this dead world?"
Rose thought all this too good to be true,
Still doubting asked, "How can I trust you?"
The woman looked to her companions,
Who showed the books that they had scavenged.
Each of them dropped bags slung on their backs,
Revealing that which bundled in sacks.
Books and books and only books their loot,
Rose looked confused but soon took in truth.
Fear dispelled when all seemed lost of grace,
Tears of joy then fell down Rose's face.
The woman, with old grey hair, hugged Rose,
A moment untold repair composed.
Rose was speechless, her luck had so chanced,
"Do you have any food?" she then asked.
"We do have food", the woman replied,
"So tell us all, you can so confide."
The woman gave Rose some bread to eat,
And lemonade to wash down some meat.
The woman then sat down next to Rose,
The others went around searching prose.
The woman had eyes of kind safety,
And-so; calming, Rose told her story.
"I was born underground, I'm sixteen,
But in the mine we began starving.
So I escaped it some days ago,
Now I await death, come what may so.

Accept, alone, above I made it",
Rose wept, "But then hope and love faded."
"My dear child", said the woman endeared,
"Your exile ends, we can give you care.
We have food and life and hopes and dreams,
We can provide these to you indeed.
A home we have; Biblioteca,
Can come with us, it is protected.
There live some nine hundred people there,
Children with smiles and prosperous years.
You can join them, go to school and learn,
And know more than cruel and cesspool hurt.
For knowledge is our redeeming light,
Our solace to other screaming life.
Man is a virus but for this light,
We can be tyrants, drunk on our 'might'.
Evil has no masters, only slaves,
People do its asking are betrayed.
Evil, at first, presents as easy,
Until, at last, defeats completely.
Ignorance is a thief to mankind,
Rigorous belief - our suicide.
Knowledge rights our worst temptations,
Alight, shining, illumination.
It's intellect that's truest power,
And gentleness the tallest tower.
To know we only know a fraction,
This is how we become perfection.
Truth is the light, exciting and grand,
Our only hope to rebuild these lands.
Books contain many things, truth and not,
But in the end they're thoughts not forgot.

So collect them all, the bad and good,
They represent a mind, personhood.
The human mind can travel in time,
Nothing can bind its unravelled heights.
Books are vessels to sail these ascents,
To reach levels unavailable then.
I have walked on surface of the Sun,
And have talked with, conversed with the One.
In the pages willing us to soar,
I have aged ten trillion years or more.
I have been with eternity's light,
And have seen absurdity's plight.
Fiction and science, Earth's poetry,
Written alliance of art and deeds.
Music plays at Biblioteca,
Magic is made, emotions tendered.
All these things await the quiet soul,
With ease, elation's pavements stroll.
So will you come with us to this place?
Oh, my apologies, what's your name?"
Rose was mesmerised by what she heard,
Spoken mystified by woman's words.
"My name is Rose", she finally said,
"And what is yours?" she asked as she wept.
"My name is also that which flowers,
The same as my mother, handed down.
Lily - though I have not seen one grow,
Tell me, have you ever seen a rose?"
Rose had no idea what she meant,
Nobody told her of flower's scent.
"What is a flower?" Rose came to ask,
And doing so, near broke Lily's heart.

"Flowers once did grow out of the ground,
The coloured rose; most famous abound.
But the soil can't give them life today,
It's been spoiled and spit in man's betray.
Except, it seems, for one last admired,
For you might be the sweetest flower.
Men dug mines to find precious metals,
But I think you're the mine's most special.
Look, it's about time we left this place,
We shouldn't be here when darkness fades.
All your questions, we can answer them,
Until when, Rose, you ask some too deep.
Then you'll have to seek your own answers,
But you'll have books to read advantage.
It's time we left this ruined city.
We ride on bikes, you can ride with me."
On the streets, on motorbikes they rode,
Knowledge thieves, with stolen writes and prose.
They rode out the Los Angeles night,
Rose hung on the back of Lily's bike.
Out into the desert sands they went,
Headlights shined the outskirt lands relent.
And soon the lights - Biblioteca,
It shone so bright out in the desert.
A refuge of light and graciousness,
A deluge of white in blackened mists.
Walls of ruins and twisted metal,
Tall, lined with snipers upper levels.
The sharp shooters saw the motorbikes,
And then the riders flashed Morse code lights.
The gates opened as they approached them,
The bikes roared in, the gates then closing.

Rose was stunned; a settlement so fine,
Rows of wonder, perfection abides.
Homes, lights, shops, and even a garden,
Glowing sights, they were the guardians.
Gentle, fragile, tender, a candle,
Settled, worthwhile, safe from bandits.
In a world of wild tears and hatred,
Here was a town of smiling faces.
Streets with people, an old thing's affair,
Broken pieces emboldened repair.
Seeing Rose, the people gathered round,
Lily introduced her to the crowds.
Rose spent some days being nursed to health,
And sent people to the mines to help.
Lily used a map to help her find,
And they reviewed her tracks to the mine.
But though they searched, they were too late,
Below the surface - a lonely grave.
Sighs of grief called into the ages,
The sky seemed to fall upon her face.
The sky pulled her heart out of her mouth,
It tried to haul it across the clouds.
The days wore on of its occurrence,
Rose mourned the passing of her parents...
Months faded to years and years did age,
And Rose matured out of teenage ways.
Out on raids for books and food she rode,
Throughout ruins looked and looted roamed.
The bandits on bikes in search for truth,
And armed with weapons and words of proof.
Lost survivors were found and rescued,
Rose reminded of her own refuge.

One such survivor was named Thomas,
And his blue eyes gave Rose a promise.
Love, first love, the greatest of Earth's things,
The thirst so-quenched latent water springs.
Before the town, Rose and Thomas wed,
And all were proud, such flawless event.
Biblioteca grew with the years,
And-so; Rose selected a career.
To hunt the world saw sights and wonder,
But studies could draw more than plunder.
So Rose left the bandit crew frontlines,
She rode her last phantom route goodbye.
And into the world of science walked,
Biology and chemistry talk.
She saw the Universe, hidden math,
Explored the unending pattern maps.
Till came the time she wanted to find,
A way for vines and plants to survive.
Biblioteca's crops grew with care,
But they could never hope to wild fare.
"If we are to rebuild our dead world,
Need flowers to fulfil and unfurl.
We need trees to breathe and clean the skies,
To seed, seep, and heave their green disguise.
It is my dream to free this science,
This I seek, seed of life's defiance."
As she toiled for years on this great quest,
Pregnant and childbirth became so-blessed.
A daughter came to her and Thomas,
Purest water, first word was, "Mama".
The years rolled on until a breakthrough,
Despair's toll gone in a moment's fuse.

Using charged ions toxicity,
She fused plants mine's electricity.
Plants could now survive without the Sun,
Chance would now give rise to them undone.
And to her part; it goes on forever,
Her super plants; echoes of an era.
For Rose would die and pass on her tune,
That life might fight and, at last; the **Bloom**.

PART V

The Bloom

The ache of ten million years went by,
Age of the human fears subsided.
Every trace of humanity gone,
They'd been erased by time's ramble on.
The burned atmosphere had been renewed,
The Earth was once more its vibrant blue.
Oceans washed and surged with power,
So-then, watch; the age of flowers.
For in the return of the old blue,
Herein was truth, truth behold; the **Bloom**.
Human hands had destroyed the landscape,
And with land gone, seas exploit reshaped.
A new intelligence soon emerged,
Ocean benevolence, truth submerged.
They survived the nuclear wasting,
By hiding in the deepest places.
Their hunger forced the most creative,
To wonder, learn, sow innovations.
Whales, gentle beasts, became the Godheads,
Oceans bequeathed and made them Goddess.
After the humans, this smarter life,
Mastered emotions of soaring lights.
Their brains growing in different ways,
Became glowing intellect attained.
Feeling and empathy their language,
Healing in symphony so tranquil.
Colours and textures of love were known,

Creatures of next phases so-bestowed.
They swam the seas in graceful grandeur,
They had the ease of peaceful saviours.
Imbued, uncurled; this last paradigm,
In blue, the world, at last, in its prime.
The world turned in slow and thinking spin,
The whales awed and flowed succinct therein.
The planet was now a floating mind,
And in it how emotions refined.
The whales never tried to leave the Earth,
Prevailed better minds to peace coerce.
Through dimensions and love they travelled,
To time's endless thereof unravelled.
Avoiding the slopes of human curse,
Anointed hosts of the Universe.
In a state of Zen and Om defined,
The planet so-went and swam aligned.
Against the backdrop of empty space,
Did sense; unique orb of sentience.
Mindful dilation being felt,
Like a pinprick against the black silk.
Entire thought shaped of this thesis orb,
One planet; an idea in form.
A speck, a dot of pure intellect,
Azteca God; the world in connect.
The zenith of Earth's billion-year drop,
Which Venus and Mars jealously watched.
And the oceans glistened blue and white,
The whales motioned, listened, bathed sunlight.
Breaching the water's surface for air,
Breathing once-slaughtered virgin's affair.
Nowhere such place of lasting features,

In all of space's vastest reaches.
A melodious call to the stars,
The harmonious era - at last.
The great peace, the timeless age of joy,
Innate sleep, the calm before the storm.
For the **Bloom** was bringing closure soon,
Resume its drumming, the flower's cue.
A second big bang, yet bang nor boom,
It beckoned became, this name; the **Bloom**.
The Earth was the inspiration stage,
Universe's incandescent rave.
Against all the odds of fate and chance,
Suspense withdrawn; clock the age of plants.
As the whales swam in wisdom oceans,
Back on the land; the flowers growing.
Descendants of Rose's volted crops,
Replenished had grown, evolved, unstopped.
For though the human's failed to rebuild,
They'd sown the healing fields of the world.
So when the very last human died,
Surrendered them under bluer skies.
But they could not regain of their place,
They had their lot, their warnings unfazed.
Fate found a new purpose for people,
Resound so-through in Rose's petals.
The plants she gave electric impulse,
Enhanced with age, synthetic signals.
Earth's revolution resolution,
Electrocution evolution!
Electric forests, magnetic air,
Connected tropics, kinetic flare.
Electron jungles with vines of volts,

Perfection's struggle designed provoke.
Reliant on the Sun nevermore,
Defiant wonder plants went galore.
These plants fed not on light but matter,
Atmosphere stopped no nighttime scatter.
These plants didn't die with lack of food,
It would just inspire their growing roots.
These plants needed not of oxygen,
Enhanced seeded lot from consequence.
They swept across the Earth unopposed,
And crept upon anything exposed.
And-so; they conquered highest mountains,
Below; they covered ocean fountains.
Whales and flowers existed in peace,
Until the hour resisted the seas.
The whales could speak with telepathy,
And willed the flowers some sympathy.
But nothing could stop their endless **Bloom**,
So the whales accepted coming doom.
Like a dreaming to the sleeping eyes,
The unthinking beauty had arrived.
All the thoughts and Zen had come to pass,
So now all that was left was to last.
For what use is there to endless time,
If not used to beautify entwine?
Come lilac, come greenheart, come daisy,
And iris and chestnut and daphne.
Come zelkova, come polyanthus,
And totara and podocarpus.
Come gardenia, come vinca minor,
Oleander, erica, alba.
Come hydrangea and come magnolia,

And impatiens and plume celosia.
Come hemlock, come pohutukawa,
Hollyhock and elm and acacia.
Come sawtooth, come palm, come narcissus,
Peppermint and gum and violet.
Come tulip and come coreopsis,
And snowdrop and walnut and cypress.
Come camphor, come anemone,
Sycamore and oak and begonia.
Come sedum, tuberose, hellebore,
Alyssum and primrose and acorn.
Come snapdragon, willow, petunia,
Jacaranda and mallow, primula.
Come mayflower, come dianella,
And moonflower and candelabra.
Come marigold and ipomoea,
Solidago and come nemesia.
Come viola, come wisteria,
And columbine and watsonia.
Come hibiscus and come nigella,
And clematis and dahlia.
Lavender, come clover, come foxglove,
Trillium and cedar and yucca.
Come redwood, come citron, come poppy,
Daffodil and orchid and lily.
And, of course, come the one most famous,
The one with all of wonder's greatness.
In promise white and every colour,
In homage likeness to their mother.
Come rose, the queen of beauty's heirloom,
Grow to lead in duty the **Bloom**.
Succulents and cacti chevaliers,

Fluorescent and fungi racketeers.
Some of these plants had stems of lightning,
These were the ones ascend the mountains.
Some of them had enormous petals,
Formed from electric pulse or metals.
Even the bowels of the Earth turned,
Lava flowers and vines emerged.
Consuming all the matter of Earth,
The **Bloom** begun; it had had its first.
Needing more matter to so devour,
Seeding spores out to plant new flowers.
And-so; soon they spread beyond the Earth,
To the Moon and across its surface.
The colours were green and red and blue,
And flowers did seed, imbed the Moon.
With collective move; remorseless **Bloom**,
Rich electric hues transformed the Moon.
So the Earth and Moon now pulsed with life,
In an ever-glowing mist of light.
Between them, a tether of light grew,
Seemed to stem together, life infused.
Tether of light pulled the worlds inwards,
Overriding gravity's orders.
And Earth and Moon then came together,
Their crash was smooth, softened magnetic.
The energy of two worlds touching,
A synergy, the **Bloom** erupting.
Like the supernovae of the stars,
Came the booming of these worlds apart.
Earth and Moon exploded in a burst,
As the **Bloom** expended them dispersed.
Using their energy for power,

Plumes of seeds launched out with the flowers.
Earth and Moon were over, journey done,
But the **Bloom** was hardly yet begun.
Flying across the solar system,
Vines and moss, the furthest distance.
The spores rained down just like the comets,
They tore across the skies in torrents.
The first planet they reached was Venus,
Atmosphere harsh but none too grievous.
The second planet they reached was Mars,
It took not long to be rich of plants.
The third planet reached was Mercury,
Plants splurged on it at once succeeded.
Mars and its small moons detonated,
Thousands of seeds soon resonated.
Venus and Mercury exploded too,
Billions of years undone by the **Bloom**.
The flow of life now so infectious,
With flowers now in all directions.
Millions of plants burned up in the Sun,
Brilliant desires but this time would come.
From the deep and soon constellations,
The next step in the **Bloom**'s invasion.
The plants soon reached the asteroid belt,
Vines and leaves being deployed throughout.
They transformed the belt into a wreath,
They adorned their beautiful conceit.
Comets smaller than the planet spheres,
It took longer to explode from here.
So a million years or so they grew,
Billions of flowers became anew.
Then these planet executioners,

Landed on the moons of Jupiter.
Seeds, traipsing in eternity's arc,
Heeded straying gravity's path.
Callisto, Europa, Ganymede,
And Io; ambrosia's many seeds.
Smaller moons were also overgrown,
Ordered soon to follow and dethrone.
The next step was the **Bloom**'s truest test,
Could it ebb Jupiter to ferment?
Communicating with each other,
Illuminated conscious ushered.
The moons all detonated at once,
And together produced enough flux.
That the gas giant world could then **Bloom**,
And the red planet unfurled in plumes.
In the unending search for matter,
Flowers that sent had soon reached Saturn.
The soaring rings of Saturn's power,
Adoring stems in patterned flowers.
And the flowers grew on Saturn's moons,
But they didn't detonate so soon.
The rings and moons encircled Saturn,
And plants did soon invert a fashion.
The plants were evolving something new,
Their dance to forever change the **Bloom**.
The plants had come to newer scatter,
By which they could use antimatter.
Around the vines of Saturn's halo,
Astound the science, atom's gallows.
Colliding particles together,
With antiparticles dissevered.
Collision to annihilation,

The forging of plant incubation.
The energy which released from this,
The plants succeeded and harnessed it.
The tree's imperial intricate;
Antimaterialsynthesis!
Magically happen; folded fern,
Gradually, Saturn whole did turn.
Saturn's giant flower spun complete,
Circled by its crowning rings and wreath.
In its slowness of wondrous verdure,
The hypnosis of rose Saturn's turn.
It was the most beautiful of sights,
One enormous electrical life.
Time's unrehearsed unfearing lotus,
The Universe, nearing its opus.
Once Saturn's flower was completed,
Her wreath and moons then detonated.
This universal moss relentless,
Its dispersal in hot momentum.
Uranus, by grace of all her moons,
Luminous and changed also to **Bloom**.
With Jupiter flowering like old,
The plants moved to Neptune and took hold.
The plants covered Titan in their life,
At once, enveloped entire astride.
And like the two planets before it,
The ripe Neptune canvas to fauna.
And when Neptune's **Bloom** was completed,
So did its moons be gone and seeded.
The plants hurled out to the depths of space,
Beyond the realm solar system's trace.
But before they would reach new planets,

Something else was about to happen.
Wreath of asteroids around the Sun,
Sent the atoms colliding begun.
The scale of what then soon unfolded,
Regale the Sun to **Bloom** beholden.
But to **Bloom** the Sun, some new power,
Evolved a way to bring it flower.
Dark matter used, consumed, and transferred,
Forgathered true then groomed and incurred.
With such abundant fertile matter,
Blush the Sun faster than the planets.
The sweeping solar flaming arches,
To breathing flower framing branches.
The flower rise, solar flare begins,
The flow of time so-near had witnessed.
It took millions of years to complete,
But the brilliant compared masterpiece.
Rosebud of fire, soaring petals grown,
Pose desire, towering revel glow.
Unshaded plant, virgin rose adorn,
In radiant worship of its form.
Ember flower of colossal size,
Splendour bestowed in blossoming times.
Sacred, precious, alive, electric,
Naked, massive, the flower's centric.
Turning in a golden slow rotate,
Burning stem and molten glow ornate.
Defining feature, life's goliath,
The shining beacon, light and triumph.
The Sun, the flower, the king of light,
The stunning hour of the bringing life.
For billions of years, the Sun had grown,

The life on Earth, cared for its condone.
But now life had reclaimed its mother,
The flowers had remade and summoned.
Then, as if at once becoming mist,
The wreath, the asteroids, pollens gift.
The ring of flowers detonated,
In all directions - pollination.
Out towards the other star systems,
With the flowers of this one shimmers.
With fronds blossoming, juniper plume,
Beyond the looming Jupiter **Bloom**.
Passing the curl of Saturn's blossom,
Passion of purple jasmine's floral.
Reaching further than Uranus **Bloom**,
Regions yearning out beyond Neptune.
Through deep realms of interstellar space,
Where none dwelled, no cellular trace.
Until at last, they made salient,
To worlds strange, distant and alien.
To new planets the plants attended,
The organic comets descending.
Tearing across atmospheres and skies,
Fearing nothing, stratospheres defied.
Some worlds had life, civilizations,
They tried to fight off these invaders.
They lost their worlds and ancient temples,
The plants merciless in potential.
For none could overcome the barrage,
One by one, they became star corsage.
Soon, planets and stars were **Bloom**ing far,
Moons, comets, the plants assuming stars.
Rippling out in growing momentum,

Tripling clouds in flowing magentas.
Until the arm of Via Lacta,
Was full of plants, electric actors.
Insatiable; their need to unfurl,
Inescapable seeded new worlds.
At the centre of the galaxy,
Epicentre of black gravity.
Supermassive black hole revolver,
Only served to make them emboldened.
To surrender a black hole to **Bloom**,
Needed newer power to be used.
The harnessing of dark energy,
And harvesting of star destinies.
As the wake of the flowers blew on,
Undertaking the power hereon.
The twirling arms of the galaxy,
Unfurling plants and dark energy.
Galactic particle collider,
Stars raced faster than light around it.
Enormous flowers crashing, spinning,
And flawless showers flash beginnings.
And the supermassive force of void,
Succumbed like the Sun did asteroids.
The black hole slowly turned into **Bloom**,
Enact whole galaxy petals plumed.
The centre of the flower was light,
And rendered the designer to life.
Petals of light and planets and stars,
Fractals of life, botanic memoirs.
Gorgeous fortress, flawless, mystified,
An enormous flower, light years wide.
But, oh! The **Bloom** was not yet finished,

And-so; resumed it undiminished.
Cue the wondrous and grand finale,
Bloom of luscious expanded valleys.
The black hole was linked to the others,
And wormholes precinct plants discovered.
A stem of the flower grew through it,
And then it could allow conduits.
The wormholes were a network entwined,
And fertile for the reworking vines.
Countless galaxies bound in flowers,
Boundless mysteries **Bloom**ing hour.
Where was the silence of empty space,
Was now the prowess of ivy's grace.
The whole Universe now one bouquet,
So-told, and dispersed with its arrange.
The flirting spell had been reimbursed,
Curtain fell on the Garden Universe.

ABOUT THE AUTHOR

David Coyle is from Wellington, New Zealand. His grandmother encouraged him to write when he was younger. Her name was Rose.

ABOUT THE PRESS

Unsolicited Press was founded in 2012 and is based in Portland, Oregon. The team seeks to publish out-of-this-world fiction, creative nonfiction, and poetry. The team refuses to accept industry standards and acquires quirky, phenomenal, and true art from authors around the world. Learn more at www.unsolicitedpress.com.

www.ingramcontent.com/pod-product-compliance
Lightning Source LLC
Chambersburg PA
CBHW020125130526
44591CB00032B/529
* 9 7 8 1 9 4 7 0 2 1 8 0 8 *